THE

HAZEL IRVINE

BIOGRAPHY

BY

CHRISTOPHER K. WILLIAMS

All rights reserved © 2024

The scanning, uploading, and disseminating of this work online or by any other means without the author's written consent is prohibited and unlawful, unless allowed by the U.S. Copyright Act of 1976. Please do not engage in or promote the electronic piracy of protected content; instead, only buy authorized paperback and electronic versions. The purpose of this publication is to offer knowledgeable and trustworthy information on the topics discussed

Table of Contents

CHAPTER 1 1

  Introduction 1

    Overview of Hazel Irvine 1

    Significance in the Broadcasting Industry 6

CHAPTER 2 12

  Early Life and Education 12

    Birth and Childhood 12

    Academic Background 15

    Early Interests in Media 18

CHAPTER 3 22

  Career Beginnings 22

    Initial Roles in Journalism 22

    Transition to Broadcasting 24

    Key Early Projects 31

CHAPTER 4 36

  Rise to Prominence 36

    Joining the BBC 36

    Milestone Achievements in Broadcasting 42

    Major Events Covered..49

CHAPTER 5 56

    Specialization in Sports Broadcasting 56

        Coverage of Olympic Games...56

        Role in Golf and Snooker Commentary.............................63

        Memorable Sports Moments...71

CHAPTER 6 78

    Personal Life 78

        Family and Relationships 78

        Hobbies and Interests Outside Broadcasting....................82

CHAPTER 7 87

    Awards and Recognition 88

        Industry Accolades...88

        Contributions to Media and Sports Broadcasting..............93

CHAPTER 8 100

    Philanthropy and Advocacy 100

        Involvement in Charitable Causes...................................100

        Advocacy for Women in Media 107

CHAPTER 9 114

Legacy and Impact 114

    Influence on Modern Broadcasting 114

    Inspirational Figure for Aspiring Journalists......................121

Conclusion 128

    Summary of Achievements 128

    Future Prospects and Ongoing Influence.........................132

CHAPTER 1

Introduction

Overview of Hazel Irvine

Hazel Irvine is a renowned Scottish sports presenter and journalist known for her versatile broadcasting career and her significant contributions to sports media. With a career spanning several decades, she has become one of the most respected figures in British sports journalism, admired for her professionalism, in-depth knowledge of various sports, and engaging on-screen presence.

Early Life and Background

Born on May 24, 1965, in St. Andrews, Scotland, Hazel Irvine grew up in the historic town known as the home of golf. This environment likely influenced her later passion for sports. Hazel attended the University of St. Andrews, where she graduated with a degree in art history. During her time at university, she developed a keen interest in sports, participating actively in athletics and student broadcasting.

Entry into Broadcasting

Hazel began her broadcasting career in the mid-1980s, gaining her first experience as a production assistant. Her early roles helped her hone her skills behind the scenes before transitioning to on-screen work. She made her debut as a presenter with Scotland Today on STV, covering a range of topics, including sports and current affairs.

Her natural flair for broadcasting and deep knowledge of sports quickly earned her recognition, leading to more prominent opportunities within the sports journalism field.

Career Highlights

Hazel's career highlights span across multiple sports and major international events, cementing her as a leading voice in sports broadcasting:

BBC Sport:

Hazel joined BBC Sport in the 1990s, becoming one of the network's most versatile presenters. She covered major sporting events, including the Olympics, the FIFA World Cup, Wimbledon, and the Masters golf tournament. Her ability to seamlessly transition between different sports showcased her adaptability and broad expertise.

Golf Coverage:

Growing up in St. Andrews, Hazel developed a lifelong connection with golf. She became a prominent presenter for golf coverage on the BBC, including the Open Championship. Her deep understanding of the sport and ability to convey its nuances made her a trusted voice for golf enthusiasts.

Olympics:

Hazel was a familiar face for Olympic viewers, hosting BBC's coverage of numerous Summer and Winter Olympic Games. Her professionalism and enthusiasm for sports shone through as she interviewed athletes and provided insights into their performances.

Snooker:

Hazel also played a significant role in popularizing snooker coverage in the UK. Her calm and measured style of presentation resonated with viewers, making her a favorite among fans of the sport.

Style and Approach

Hazel Irvine is celebrated for her engaging and authoritative presentation style. Her ability to connect with viewers, combined with her thorough preparation and deep understanding of the sports she covers, has set her apart in the competitive world of broadcasting. She brings a sense of warmth and relatability to her coverage while maintaining a high level of professionalism.

Awards and Recognition

Over the course of her career, Hazel has received numerous accolades and recognition for her contributions to sports broadcasting. She is particularly admired for breaking barriers as a woman in a field historically dominated by men. Her work has paved the way for future generations of female sports presenters.

Personal Life and Interests

Despite her public profile, Hazel Irvine is known for maintaining a low-key personal life. She has kept much of her private life out of the spotlight, focusing instead on her career and passion for sports. Outside of broadcasting, Hazel enjoys playing golf and has remained connected to her Scottish roots. She is also known for her philanthropic work and support for sports development initiatives.

Legacy

Hazel Irvine's legacy lies in her exceptional career and her role as a trailblazer in sports journalism. She has inspired countless aspiring broadcasters with her dedication, expertise, and ability to excel across a wide range of sports. Her professionalism and authenticity continue to make her a respected figure in the industry.

Today, Hazel Irvine is regarded as one of the most accomplished and influential sports broadcasters in the UK, leaving an indelible mark on the world of sports media.

Significance in the Broadcasting Industry

Hazel Irvine holds a prominent place in the broadcasting industry, celebrated for her versatility, professionalism, and trailblazing contributions to sports media. Over her career, she has become a respected figure who has shaped how sports are covered and consumed in the UK and beyond. Her significance lies in her ability to excel across diverse sports, break barriers for women in broadcasting, and set a high standard for journalistic integrity and expertise.

1. A Trailblazer for Women in Sports Broadcasting

Hazel Irvine entered the broadcasting industry at a time when sports journalism was predominantly male-dominated. Through her exceptional talent, she broke through these barriers, becoming a trusted voice in a field where women were often underrepresented.

By hosting high-profile events such as the Olympics, the FIFA World Cup, and the Open Championship, Hazel paved the way for other women to enter and excel in sports journalism. Her success challenged stereotypes and demonstrated that women could not only participate in but lead coverage of traditionally male-dominated sports like football, snooker, and golf.

2. Versatility Across Sports and Formats

One of Hazel's most notable achievements is her ability to seamlessly cover a wide array of sports. From golf and snooker to athletics and the Olympics, Hazel has shown an extraordinary range of expertise. Her adaptability allowed her to connect with audiences across different sports and formats, from live event coverage to studio hosting and athlete interviews.

Her knowledge and passion for sports were evident in every broadcast, and her ability to engage both casual viewers and dedicated fans contributed significantly to her popularity. Few broadcasters have demonstrated such depth and versatility, cementing Hazel's reputation as one of the finest in the industry.

3. A Trusted Voice in Sports Coverage

Hazel Irvine's calm and authoritative on-screen presence made her a trusted figure in sports broadcasting. Audiences relied on her insights, analysis, and interviews during some of the most significant moments in sports history. Her professionalism and attention to detail ensured accurate and engaging coverage, helping viewers feel more connected to the events they were watching.

Her work during the Olympics, for instance, exemplified her ability to bring context, emotion, and understanding to complex sporting events, ensuring that global audiences could appreciate the stories and achievements of the athletes.

4. Champion of Golf Broadcasting

As a native of St. Andrews, the "home of golf," Hazel Irvine's connection to the sport is deeply personal. Her extensive work covering golf tournaments, particularly the Open Championship and the Masters, established her as a leading voice in golf broadcasting. Her ability to articulate the nuances of the sport and convey its rich history made her coverage appealing to both seasoned golf enthusiasts and newcomers. Hazel's presence helped elevate the profile of golf broadcasting and brought greater attention to the sport on mainstream platforms.

5. Key Contributor to the BBC's Sports Legacy

Hazel Irvine has been a cornerstone of the BBC's sports coverage for decades, contributing to its reputation as a leading broadcaster of global sporting events. Her involvement in landmark events like the Olympics, FIFA World Cups,

Wimbledon, and the Commonwealth Games showcased the BBC's commitment to excellence, with Hazel often serving as the face of these broadcasts.

Her professionalism and expertise became synonymous with the BBC's sports brand, reinforcing its standing as a trusted source for high-quality coverage. Hazel's long-standing association with the network underscored her importance to its legacy and influence in the broadcasting world.

6. Inspirational Figure for Aspiring Broadcasters

Through her career, Hazel has inspired countless aspiring journalists and broadcasters. Her journey from regional television to global sports events serves as a testament to her hard work, dedication, and talent. Her ability to balance in-depth knowledge, professionalism, and relatability has set a standard for excellence in sports broadcasting.

Aspiring broadcasters look to Hazel as a role model for navigating a highly competitive industry while staying true to one's passion and values. Her legacy is not just in her on-screen work but also in the path she has cleared for the next generation.

7. Elevating the Perception of Sports Journalism

Hazel Irvine has played a pivotal role in elevating the perception of sports journalism. Her in-depth analysis, insightful interviews, and articulate delivery brought greater credibility and respect to the profession. She demonstrated that sports journalism is not just about reporting scores but about telling compelling stories, analyzing intricate strategies, and celebrating the human spirit.

Her work has helped to blur the lines between sports and broader cultural conversations, emphasizing the significance of sports as a unifying and inspiring force in society.

8. Advocacy for Inclusion in Sports Media

While Hazel Irvine is not overtly political, her career itself stands as a quiet advocacy for greater inclusivity in sports media. By excelling in her field and refusing to be confined by traditional gender expectations, she has contributed to a more inclusive and diverse broadcasting landscape. Her success underscores the importance of representation and the value of diverse voices in shaping how sports are understood and appreciated.

CHAPTER 2

Early Life and Education

Birth and Childhood

Hazel Irvine was born on May 24, 1965, in the historic town of St. Andrews, Fife, Scotland. Known worldwide as the "home of golf," St. Andrews likely played a formative role in shaping Hazel's lifelong connection to sports, particularly golf.

Growing up in a small Scottish town surrounded by a rich sporting culture, Hazel developed an early appreciation for outdoor activities and athleticism. Her family encouraged her active lifestyle and supported her interests in various sports. She often participated in school competitions, showcasing an early talent for athletics and team-based activities.

A Love for Sports and Curiosity

Hazel's childhood was characterized by an innate curiosity and a love for sports. St. Andrews, with its iconic golf courses and vibrant sporting community, provided a unique environment that fueled her passion. Although her interests extended beyond golf to include other athletic pursuits like running and team sports, the town's emphasis on the sport left an indelible mark on her.

Hazel's upbringing in this idyllic Scottish setting instilled in her a sense of discipline and a drive to excel, traits that would later define her career in sports broadcasting.

Education and Early Interests

From a young age, Hazel displayed a keen intellect and a wide range of interests. Alongside her athletic endeavors, she excelled academically and demonstrated a talent for storytelling and communication. These qualities laid the foundation for her future career as a broadcaster, where her ability to blend knowledge, passion, and relatability would become her trademark.

Her childhood in St. Andrews not only nurtured her love for sports but also instilled a strong sense of identity and pride in her Scottish roots. These elements would later influence her professional journey and the unique perspective she brought to her work in sports journalism.

Academic Background

Hazel Irvine's academic journey reflects her intellectual curiosity and diverse interests, which would later shape her multifaceted career in broadcasting. She pursued her education with a balance of academic rigor and extracurricular involvement, particularly in sports and communication, laying the groundwork for her future in sports journalism.

Schooling in Scotland

Hazel attended local schools in her hometown of St. Andrews, where she was known for her academic diligence and active participation in extracurricular activities. Her natural aptitude for communication and storytelling became evident during her school years, as did her enthusiasm for sports. Her schooling provided her with a strong foundation in critical thinking and public speaking, skills that would prove essential in her broadcasting career.

University Education

Hazel Irvine attended the University of St. Andrews, one of Scotland's most prestigious institutions. She graduated with a degree in Art History, a field that may seem unrelated to sports broadcasting but equipped her with a keen analytical mind and an appreciation for cultural narratives. Studying art history honed her ability to synthesize information, present compelling narratives, and develop a broad cultural perspective skills that she would later apply to her career as a journalist and presenter.

Involvement in University Sports

While pursuing her degree, Hazel actively participated in university sports, showcasing her athletic abilities and fostering a deeper connection to the sporting world. She was involved in athletics, including field hockey and running, which further deepened her understanding of teamwork, discipline, and competition.

Her active participation in sports during her university years not only fueled her passion but also provided her with firsthand experience of the challenges and triumphs faced by athletes a perspective she carried into her broadcasting career.

Broadcasting Experience at University

Hazel's interest in communication and storytelling found an outlet during her time at university, where she began to explore broadcasting. She took part in student-led media initiatives, developing her skills in presenting, interviewing, and reporting.

These early experiences in university broadcasting gave her a taste of the media industry and solidified her ambition to pursue a career in journalism, specifically within the realm of sports.

Continued Education and Development

Hazel Irvine's academic background is complemented by her commitment to lifelong learning and professional development. Throughout her career, she demonstrated an ability to adapt to changing trends in media and sports journalism, showcasing a dedication to staying informed and relevant in her field.

Early Interests in Media

Hazel Irvine's early interests in media were sparked during her formative years, combining her natural talent for communication with her passion for storytelling. These interests, nurtured throughout her education and extracurricular activities, laid the foundation for her future career in sports broadcasting.

Influence of Storytelling and Communication

From a young age, Hazel exhibited a knack for expressing herself clearly and confidently, traits that often drew her toward opportunities involving public speaking and storytelling. She enjoyed engaging with others, whether through school presentations or casual discussions about sports and current events. This natural inclination toward communication hinted at her potential for a career in media.

Exposure to Media and Broadcasting

Growing up in St. Andrews, Hazel was exposed to a variety of local and national media, including television broadcasts of major sporting events. Watching professional broadcasters seamlessly convey complex sports narratives intrigued her and inspired her to consider a role in media.

The environment of her hometown, steeped in sporting history, further fueled her interest in sports reporting. Golf tournaments and local events provided her with early exposure to the intersection of sports and media, leaving a lasting impression.

Extracurricular Involvement in Communication

During her school and university years, Hazel sought out opportunities to explore her interest in media. She participated in student-led initiatives, such as debate clubs and campus broadcasting projects, where she practiced public speaking, reporting, and presentation skills. These experiences gave her a practical understanding of how media could amplify stories, particularly those related to sports.

University Media Projects

While studying art history at the University of St. Andrews, Hazel expanded her engagement with media. She contributed to student-run media outlets, covering topics ranging from campus news to sports events. These projects allowed her to experiment with different formats, from interviews to live event commentary, and provided her with invaluable hands-on experience.

Combining Media and Sports Passion

Hazel's early interests in media were deeply intertwined with her passion for sports. Her active involvement in athletics gave her a unique perspective on the challenges and triumphs of athletes, which she skillfully translated into her reporting. Recognizing the power of media to bring sports stories to life, she decided to pursue a career that would allow her to combine her love for both fields.

CHAPTER 3

Career Beginnings

Initial Roles in Journalism

Hazel Irvine's entry into journalism marked the beginning of a distinguished career characterized by versatility, professionalism, and a deep passion for storytelling. Her early roles in journalism served as a training ground where she developed the skills and experience that would later make her one of the most respected figures in sports broadcasting.

Early Career Beginnings

Hazel began her professional journey in the mid-1980s, shortly after graduating from the University of St. Andrews with a degree in art history. She started as a production assistant, working behind the scenes to gain an understanding of the broadcasting industry. This role allowed her to familiarize herself with the technical aspects of television production, including editing, scripting, and coordinating live broadcasts.

Her first major on-screen opportunity came with STV (Scottish Television), where she worked as a reporter and presenter for Scotland Today. This position required her to cover a wide range of topics, from current affairs to human interest stories, providing her with valuable experience in journalistic versatility.

Focus on Sports Journalism

Hazel's love for sports soon guided her toward specializing in sports journalism. She took on roles that allowed her to report on local and national sporting events, showcasing her ability to analyze games and conduct interviews with athletes and coaches. Her growing expertise in sports reporting caught the attention of industry professionals, leading to opportunities to cover high-profile events. Hazel's engaging style, combined with her in-depth knowledge of various sports, quickly set her apart from her peers.

Freelance Work and Skill Development

In her early career, Hazel also took on freelance assignments, working with different media outlets to broaden her experience. These roles helped her refine her skills in live reporting, event coverage, and feature writing. The variety of assignments allowed her to adapt to different audiences and formats, making her a well-rounded journalist.

Key Breakthroughs

Hazel's breakthrough in sports journalism came when she was selected to cover major sporting events for larger networks. Her ability to provide insightful commentary and her calm demeanor under pressure earned her recognition within the industry. She began to establish herself as a trusted voice in sports media, paving the way for her transition to national and international platforms.

Transition to Broadcasting

Hazel Irvine's transition into broadcasting was marked by a series of early career moves that showcased her natural talents, persistence, and dedication to her craft. Unlike many in the industry who followed traditional routes, Hazel's path into sports journalism was both unique and gradual, relying on her ability to learn on the job and adapt to the fast-paced world of television production.

Early Career and Entry into Broadcasting

Hazel's journey into broadcasting began after she graduated with a degree in Art History from the University of St. Andrews. While her academic background was not directly related to journalism or broadcasting, her university years were pivotal in shaping her career interests. At St. Andrews, Hazel became involved in sports, particularly athletics, and began to develop an understanding of the sports world. This involvement not only helped her gain confidence but also fueled her desire to pursue a career in broadcasting.

Initially, Hazel's role in broadcasting wasn't on screen. She started her career behind the scenes, gaining invaluable experience as a production assistant at local Scottish television station, STV. During this time, she developed a strong understanding of how television programs were produced and the logistical side of live events, which would later serve her well when transitioning to on-screen roles.

First On-Screen Opportunities

Hazel's first break into presenting came with the local Scottish news program Scotland Today, where she was tasked with reporting on various topics, including sports. Her presenting style quickly gained attention, and it was clear that she had the poise and communication skills needed for a broader audience. This early exposure to presenting news and sports marked the beginning of Hazel's transition from behind the camera to a more visible and public-facing role.

Her growing confidence and ability to engage viewers led to more prominent opportunities within the broadcasting industry, including national and international sports coverage. Hazel's early training in both the technical and presentation aspects of television allowed her to move seamlessly into more significant roles as a sports presenter.

Joining BBC Sport

Hazel's big break in sports broadcasting came when she joined BBC Sport in the 1990s. Her role with the BBC signaled a new chapter in her career, allowing her to cover a wide range of sporting events, including high-profile competitions such as the FIFA World Cup, Wimbledon, the Olympic Games, and major golf and snooker tournaments.

At the BBC, Hazel quickly gained a reputation for her calm, authoritative delivery and deep knowledge of sports. Her transition into sports journalism was not only marked by her ability to present events with clarity and insight but also her skill in providing expert commentary on technical aspects of sports. Hazel's sports knowledge, combined with her engaging presenting style, enabled her to effectively communicate with a broad range of audiences from casual viewers to hardcore fans.

Expanding Her Role Across Various Sports

One of the standout features of Hazel's transition into broadcasting was her ability to diversify her portfolio across multiple sports. In a time when many broadcasters specialized in a single sport, Hazel made a name for herself by covering a wide array of events with authority and enthusiasm. She worked extensively in golf, becoming a regular face on BBC's coverage of The Open Championship and other prestigious golf tournaments. Her deep connection to golf, nurtured by her upbringing in St. Andrews, made her a natural fit for covering the sport, and her insightful commentary and knowledge helped raise the profile of golf broadcasts.

Hazel's versatility also extended to snooker, where she provided coverage for major events like the World Snooker Championship. Her understanding of the game's technicalities and her ability to explain the intricacies of snooker to viewers contributed to making the sport more accessible to a broader audience. In addition to these sports, Hazel covered football, athletics, and the Olympics, which only solidified her standing as one of the most versatile and trusted sports broadcasters in the UK.

Establishing a Reputation in Olympic Broadcasting

Perhaps one of the most defining aspects of Hazel's broadcasting career is her coverage of the Olympic Games. Hazel first covered the Olympics for the BBC in the 1990s, and she continued to be a key figure in their coverage for both Summer and Winter Games. The Olympics, with their enormous scope and global significance, required broadcasters to juggle a multitude of events and storylines, and Hazel's ability to maintain composure while providing insightful commentary made her a standout presence.

Her transition to Olympic broadcasting was particularly important because it placed her in the spotlight during some of the most prestigious and watched events in the world. Her professionalism, ability to manage live coverage, and natural chemistry with fellow presenters and athletes helped cement her position as a trusted figure in Olympic coverage.

Overcoming Challenges and Embracing Growth

Hazel's transition into broadcasting also involved overcoming the challenges many women face in male-dominated industries like sports journalism. Her ability to rise above any potential skepticism and prove her worth as both a presenter and expert commentator is a testament to her skill and determination. Hazel's success opened doors for other women in sports broadcasting, breaking down barriers and showing that expertise, charisma, and professionalism are key to succeeding in the field, regardless of gender.

Throughout her career, Hazel embraced opportunities for growth and continued learning. Her transition from local news reporting to national and international sports presenting was marked by a constant commitment to expanding her knowledge and improving her skills.

figure in sports journalism, inspiring future broadcasters with her pioneering path from production assistant to sports media icon.

Key Early Projects

Hazel Irvine's career in broadcasting began with several formative roles that laid the foundation for her later success as a leading sports presenter. These early projects not only helped establish her credibility but also provided her with the skills and experience necessary to make a lasting impact on British sports journalism.

1. Scotland Today (Late 1980s – Early 1990s)

One of Hazel's first significant on-screen roles was with the Scottish television program Scotland Today on STV (Scottish Television). Here, she began her broadcasting career, gaining experience presenting a variety of topics, including news and sports. This role allowed her to develop her presenting skills and understand the dynamics of television production. Though initially involved in general news reporting, it was her coverage of sports stories that garnered the most attention and set the stage for her future in sports broadcasting.

2. BBC Reporting and Early Appearances (1990s)

In the early 1990s, Hazel made her first appearances on BBC Sport, which marked a major turning point in her career. She was a part of the BBC team that covered major sporting events, including football, athletics, and rugby. These early appearances gave Hazel the chance to refine her skills in live sports broadcasting. Her calm demeanor, clear communication style, and ability to break down complex events in real time helped her quickly gain recognition in the industry.

3. The Open Championship (1990s)

Hazel's association with golf specifically The Open Championship became one of the defining early projects of her career. Growing up in St. Andrews, Hazel had a personal connection to golf, which translated into a natural and authoritative presence when covering the sport. She was part of the BBC's team for the Open, one of the most prestigious tournaments in golf. Her deep knowledge of the game and ability to explain the intricacies of golf to viewers helped elevate the sport's profile on British television. This project was critical in establishing her as a credible and knowledgeable voice in sports broadcasting.

4. Coverage of the 1994 FIFA World Cup

In 1994, Hazel Irvine covered the FIFA World Cup for the BBC. This event marked a significant milestone in her career, as the World Cup was one of the most-watched sporting events globally. Hazel's ability to navigate the high-pressure environment of live sports coverage and her engaging presenting style helped her stand out. Her role in this project was key in broadening her reputation beyond the UK, as she became a recognized face in global sports broadcasting.

5. BBC's Coverage of the 1996 Olympic Games

Hazel Irvine's role in covering the 1996 Summer Olympics in Atlanta was another crucial early project in her career. The Olympics are one of the most demanding events for sports broadcasters, as they involve multiple disciplines and a constant flow of live action. Hazel's ability to manage the live coverage of these events, conduct interviews with athletes, and provide insightful commentary under intense scrutiny marked her as a standout talent. The success of her work during the Olympics demonstrated her capacity to handle large-scale sports events with professionalism and skill.

6. BBC Snooker Coverage (1990s – Early 2000s)

Hazel's involvement in snooker coverage for the BBC, particularly during the World Snooker Championship, was another key project that helped establish her career. Snooker, with its often technical nature, required a broadcaster who could explain the rules and strategies clearly while keeping the audience engaged. Hazel's calm and approachable presenting style made her a perfect fit for this project. She became a trusted figure in the snooker community, and her coverage was praised for making the sport more accessible to wider audiences.

7. Grandstand (1990s)

Hazel also contributed to the BBC's iconic sports program Grandstand, which was one of the longest-running sports shows in British television history. Grandstand provided coverage of various sports events, from athletics to rugby, and Hazel became a familiar face on the program. Her work on Grandstand helped her build a solid reputation as a capable and knowledgeable presenter who could handle a range of different sports. This project exposed her to a large, diverse audience and was integral in cementing her status as a prominent sports broadcaster.

CHAPTER 4

Rise to Prominence

Joining the BBC

Hazel Irvine's transition to the BBC marked a pivotal moment in her career, setting her on a trajectory that would see her become one of the UK's most prominent sports broadcasters. Her move to the BBC in the early 1990s not only amplified her career but also established her as a key figure in the realm of sports journalism. Below is a detailed look at Hazel's journey to the BBC and her early contributions to the network.

The Move to BBC Sport (Early 1990s)

In the early 1990s, Hazel Irvine made a decisive move from regional television to the BBC, the UK's national broadcaster. Having honed her skills and built a reputation at Scottish Television (STV), Hazel was offered the opportunity to join BBC Sport, a decision that would mark the beginning of her long and successful career with the network. At the time, BBC Sport was the leading broadcaster of major sporting events in the UK, and joining the team provided Hazel with the chance to work at the highest level of sports media.

Early Roles at BBC Sport

Upon joining the BBC, Hazel began working as a presenter and reporter for a range of sports, covering events such as athletics, rugby, and football. She quickly gained recognition for her professional and approachable style, which made her a natural fit for the network's sports coverage. Her early roles included presenting on Grandstand, the BBC's flagship sports program, which featured live broadcasts of a variety of events, from football to tennis and everything in between. This exposure helped Hazel establish herself as a trusted face of sports broadcasting in the UK.

Becoming a Recognized Voice for Major Sporting Events

The early years at the BBC saw Hazel become a regular presence on coverage of key sporting events. One of her earliest assignments was covering the 1994 FIFA World Cup. As part of the BBC's World Cup team, Hazel brought clarity, knowledge, and enthusiasm to her coverage, which was widely praised by viewers.

Her professionalism, combined with her approachable manner, made her a standout broadcaster, and her ability to adapt to different sports further cemented her growing reputation.

Hazel also became involved in snooker coverage, particularly during the World Snooker Championship, a role that would later become one of her signature contributions to BBC Sport. As a presenter for snooker events, she demonstrated her capacity to convey the complexities of the game in an accessible and engaging way, helping to broaden the sport's appeal to a larger audience.

Coverage of the Olympics

One of the key moments of Hazel's early years at the BBC came in 1996 when she was selected to cover the Olympic Games in Atlanta. The Olympics, with its broad array of sporting events and massive global audience, required broadcasters to manage live coverage, conduct interviews, and offer insightful commentary. Hazel's role in these broadcasts allowed her to showcase her versatility as a presenter. Whether it was handling the fast-paced environment of track and field or offering analysis on more niche sports, Hazel's clear communication and calm demeanor earned her widespread recognition as a trusted voice for Olympic coverage.

Building a Reputation for Versatility

Hazel's versatility became one of her defining traits as she worked across a variety of sports and programming formats. She presented live sports, conducted interviews with athletes, and anchored sports documentaries for the BBC. Her ability to balance live event coverage with in-depth analysis and behind-the-scenes reporting made her a multi-faceted asset to BBC Sport. Hazel's range extended from high-profile sports like football and tennis to more niche events such as golf and snooker, making her a well-rounded sports broadcaster with appeal across diverse fanbases.

A Familiar Face at Major Events

As the years went on, Hazel Irvine became a fixture at major sports events, most notably in her coverage of The Open Championship, the Masters, and the World Snooker Championship. Her calm yet authoritative delivery, combined with her deep understanding of these sports, made her a trusted presence for audiences watching at home. Hazel's deep connection with golf, particularly through her upbringing in St. Andrews, gave her an added layer of credibility when presenting the sport.

Her role at the BBC, particularly her work during live sports broadcasts, established her as one of the leading sports presenters in the UK. By the late 1990s and early 2000s, Hazel had become one of the network's go-to sports broadcasters, anchoring coverage of events as varied as Wimbledon, the World Cup, and the Olympics.

Impact and Legacy

Joining the BBC marked the beginning of Hazel Irvine's ascension to one of the most respected figures in British sports broadcasting. Her ability to communicate complex sports events to a broad audience while maintaining professionalism and warmth made her a beloved figure among viewers. Hazel's early work with the BBC helped break down barriers for women in sports journalism and opened doors for others to follow in her footsteps. She remains an icon within the BBC and the wider broadcasting industry, a testament to the high standards she set and the legacy she continues to build.

Milestone Achievements in Broadcasting

Hazel Irvine's career in broadcasting has been marked by a series of significant achievements that have established her as one of the most respected and influential sports presenters in the UK. From her early days at the BBC to her role in covering global sporting events, Hazel has earned a reputation for her professionalism, versatility, and enduring commitment to the world of sports journalism. Below are some of the key milestones in Hazel Irvine's career.

1. Joining BBC Sport (Early 1990s)

One of the most important milestones in Hazel Irvine's career was her decision to join BBC Sport in the early 1990s. The move from local Scottish television to the UK's national broadcaster was a pivotal moment, allowing her to step into the limelight and cover major sporting events on a much larger scale. As part of the BBC's sports team, Hazel quickly became a regular presence on national broadcasts, covering everything from football and athletics to snooker and golf.

2. Coverage of Major Global Events: The 1994 FIFA World Cup

Hazel's role as a presenter for the 1994 FIFA World Cup was a defining achievement in her early broadcasting career. Her work on the World Cup not only raised her profile within the UK but also introduced her to a global audience. With football being one of the most widely followed sports, Hazel's calm yet engaging style helped set the tone for the BBC's extensive coverage of the tournament. Her ability to provide insightful commentary and seamlessly navigate the high-pressure environment of live sports broadcasting made her a trusted presence for football fans.

3. Hosting BBC's Coverage of the 1996 Olympic Games in Atlanta

In 1996, Hazel Irvine was selected as part of the BBC team to cover the Summer Olympic Games in Atlanta, marking a significant milestone in her career. The Olympics, as one of the world's largest sporting events, posed numerous challenges, from managing live broadcasts to providing in-depth analysis. Hazel's ability to handle the complexity of covering multiple events across a two-week period, while maintaining clear communication with viewers, solidified her as one of the BBC's top sports presenters. Her coverage of the

Olympics showcased her versatility and ability to engage with a broad range of sports, from track and field to gymnastics.

4. Becoming a Fixture in Golf Broadcasting (The Open Championship, Masters)

Hazel's deep personal connection with golf, having grown up in St. Andrews, played a crucial role in her success as one of the leading golf presenters for the BBC. Her coverage of prestigious events like The Open Championship and the Masters became a cornerstone of her career. Hazel's authoritative yet approachable presenting style, coupled with her in-depth knowledge of the sport, earned her widespread recognition and made her a key figure in British golf broadcasting. Her work in golf allowed her to reach new audiences and expand her reputation as a versatile broadcaster capable of covering both high-profile and niche sports.

5. Reporting from Iconic Sporting Events: Wimbledon and World Snooker Championship

Another major achievement in Hazel Irvine's career was her involvement in the BBC's coverage of Wimbledon and the World Snooker Championship. These events are two of the UK's most-watched and beloved sports tournaments, and Hazel's role in covering them demonstrated her ability to handle some of the most prestigious and high-profile sports broadcasts. Her calm, professional presence during Wimbledon, coupled with her expert analysis of snooker during the World Snooker Championship, solidified her as a well-rounded sports broadcaster with a wealth of experience in both live event coverage and sports analysis.

6. Becoming the Face of BBC's Sports Presenting Team

By the late 1990s and early 2000s, Hazel Irvine had become one of the most trusted faces in BBC Sport. Her regular presence on programs like Grandstand and Sportscene, as well as her involvement in covering major events like the Olympics, World Cup, and The Open, made her a household name. Hazel's ability to present live sports events with clarity and insight, combined with her warm and approachable style, earned her widespread admiration. She became synonymous with BBC Sport, and her growing influence made her a key figure in shaping the network's sports coverage.

7. Long-Term Coverage of the Olympic Games

Hazel's long-term involvement in the Olympic Games, spanning multiple editions of the Summer and Winter Olympics, has been one of the most notable achievements of her career. She has been a key member of the BBC's Olympic team for over two decades, covering both the Summer and Winter Games. Hazel's role as a presenter and commentator allowed her to become one of the most familiar faces of Olympic broadcasting in the UK. Her coverage ranged from athletics to ice hockey, showcasing her ability to report on a variety of events and adapt to the unique dynamics of the Olympics. Her expertise and professionalism during the Olympics further cemented her legacy as a leading sports broadcaster.

8. Award Recognition and Public Acclaim

Over the years, Hazel Irvine has received numerous awards and accolades for her contributions to sports broadcasting. These awards reflect not only her skill as a presenter but also her influence on the broader broadcasting landscape. Hazel's recognition within the industry speaks to her sustained excellence, as she has continued to garner respect for her insightful commentary, professionalism, and ability to handle high-pressure situations. Her career achievements are a testament to her enduring impact on the sports media world.

9. Pioneering Female Presence in Sports Broadcasting

In an era where female sports broadcasters were relatively rare, Hazel Irvine became a pioneering figure for women in sports journalism. Her consistent presence in high-profile sports events and her ability to break down barriers for women in broadcasting is a landmark achievement in itself.

Hazel's success helped pave the way for future generations of female broadcasters, who now look to her as both an inspiration and a trailblazer in a traditionally male-dominated industry.

10. Celebrated Legacy as a Trusted Sports Presenter

Hazel Irvine's legacy as one of the most trusted and respected sports presenters in the UK is a monumental achievement in itself. Over the decades, she has remained a constant figure in the world of British sports broadcasting, and her ability to evolve with the changing landscape of sports media has kept her relevant and respected. Her contributions to BBC Sport and her role in bringing sports into the homes of millions of viewers make her one of the defining figures in the history of UK broadcasting.

Major Events Covered

Hazel Irvine's career in sports broadcasting has seen her cover some of the most iconic and globally recognized sporting events. Over the years, she has become synonymous with high-profile events, providing expert commentary, live updates, and in-depth analysis to millions of viewers. Below is a detailed list of some of the major events Hazel Irvine has covered throughout her illustrious career:

1. The FIFA World Cup

Hazel Irvine played a significant role in the BBC's coverage of the FIFA World Cup, one of the world's largest and most-watched sporting events. She was part of the BBC team during the 1994 FIFA World Cup in the United States, where her insightful analysis and calm presenting style helped bring the excitement of the tournament to British audiences. Her involvement in the World Cup helped cement her as one of the top sports broadcasters in the UK.

2. The Olympic Games (Summer and Winter)

One of Hazel Irvine's defining career milestones has been her long-term involvement with the Olympic Games. She has been a key member of the BBC team covering multiple Summer and Winter Olympics since the 1990s. Hazel has anchored coverage, provided in-depth interviews with athletes, and presented live updates across a wide variety of sports. Her involvement in the 1996 Atlanta Olympics, the 2000 Sydney Olympics, and the 2012 London Olympics was particularly significant, showcasing her ability to handle the vast and diverse scope of the Games.

Hazel's coverage has spanned everything from track and field and swimming to ice hockey and figure skating, making her one of the BBC's most versatile presenters during the Olympics. Her ability to engage viewers in multiple sports during the Games further solidified her reputation as a leading sports broadcaster.

3. The Open Championship

As a presenter with a personal connection to golf having grown up in St. Andrews, one of the sport's most famous locations Hazel Irvine became a key figure in the BBC's coverage of The Open Championship. Her authoritative yet approachable style made her a trusted voice for one of golf's oldest and most prestigious tournaments. Hazel has covered The Open for several years, providing live updates, interviews with players, and detailed commentary on the tournament's progress. Her long-standing involvement in golf broadcasting helped bring the sport to a broader audience in the UK.

4. Wimbledon

Wimbledon, one of the world's most prestigious tennis tournaments, has been another major event that Hazel Irvine has covered for the BBC. Known for her calm and composed presenting style, Hazel has anchored live coverage of the matches, conducted interviews with players, and offered expert analysis throughout the tournament. Hazel's involvement in Wimbledon further showcased her versatility as a broadcaster, as she seamlessly transitioned between live sports coverage and in-depth commentary on the game's strategy and player dynamics.

5. The Masters (Golf)

In addition to The Open Championship, Hazel has been a prominent figure in the BBC's coverage of The Masters one of golf's most famous and eagerly anticipated events. Hazel's knowledge of golf, coupled with her authoritative yet engaging presenting style, has made her an integral part of the BBC's coverage of this prestigious event. Her role in covering The Masters is an example of how Hazel has helped elevate the profile of golf broadcasting in the UK.

6. The World Snooker Championship

Another major event that Hazel Irvine has become synonymous with is the World Snooker Championship. She has been involved in covering the event for many years, presenting live updates and offering expert commentary on the intricacies of snooker. Her calm and knowledgeable delivery made her a trusted voice for fans of the sport, and she played a key role in making snooker more accessible to a wider audience. Hazel's contributions to the BBC's snooker coverage are highly regarded, and she remains a fixture in the sport's media landscape.

7. Commonwealth Games

Hazel has also contributed to the BBC's coverage of the Commonwealth Games, a major multi-sport event that features athletes from across the Commonwealth of Nations. Hazel's role in covering the Commonwealth Games showcased her ability to present a wide range of sports and provided her with the opportunity to engage with athletes and teams from around the world. The Commonwealth Games' diverse events, including athletics, swimming, gymnastics, and more, gave Hazel a platform to display her versatility as a sports broadcaster.

8. The Six Nations Championship (Rugby)

As a rugby enthusiast and seasoned sports presenter, Hazel Irvine has been involved in the Six Nations Championship, one of rugby's most prestigious tournaments. Hazel's coverage of the

Six Nations has included both men's and women's rugby, where she has provided live updates, analysis, and interviews with key players and coaches. Her insightful commentary and ability to cover rugby's fast-paced action with precision made her an ideal fit for this tournament, helping to increase the tournament's visibility among British audiences.

9. The Ryder Cup (Golf)

The Ryder Cup, one of the most celebrated golf events in the world, has also been part of Hazel Irvine's extensive broadcasting resume. Hazel's involvement in covering the Ryder Cup has further cemented her status as a leading golf broadcaster in the UK. As part of the BBC team, she provided live coverage, interviews, and analysis of one of the most dramatic team events in the sport of golf. Her knowledge and passion for the sport, combined with her ability to connect with viewers, have made her an important figure in the coverage of the Ryder Cup.

10. BBC Sport's Major Sporting Events Coverage

In addition to the aforementioned events, Hazel has been an integral part of the BBC's coverage of other major sporting events, including the European Football Championship (Euro 96), the World Athletics Championships, and various Premier League football matches. She has also covered Formula 1 racing, British Open tennis, and several international rugby events. Hazel's widespread involvement in such diverse sporting events speaks to her versatility and expertise as a broadcaster capable of handling various formats and sports.

CHAPTER 5

Specialization in Sports Broadcasting

Coverage of Olympic Games

Hazel Irvine has been one of the most recognizable faces in the BBC's coverage of the Olympic Games, having provided in-depth, insightful commentary, and expert analysis for multiple editions of both the Summer and Winter Olympics. Her experience covering the Olympics spans decades, and she has become synonymous with the event for British viewers. Below is a detailed overview of Hazel Irvine's involvement in the Olympic Games and her contributions to the BBC's coverage.

1. Early Involvement in Olympic Broadcasting (1990s)

Hazel Irvine's involvement in Olympic coverage began in the 1990s, marking the start of a long-standing relationship between Hazel and the BBC's Olympic broadcasting team. Her early coverage of the 1996 Summer Olympics in Atlanta helped establish her as a reliable and insightful presenter. Hazel's role during this Olympic Games was pivotal in bringing detailed and informative commentary to a British audience, as the event was held in a different time zone. Her ability to offer real-time updates, conduct engaging interviews, and provide analysis of a wide variety of sports set the tone for her future Olympic coverage.

2. The 2000 Sydney Olympics

Hazel Irvine's coverage of the 2000 Sydney Olympics was another landmark moment in her career. She played an essential role in the BBC's extensive coverage, which included live broadcasts and behind-the-scenes insights into the Games. Sydney's multi-sport nature, with events such as athletics, swimming, gymnastics, and rowing, required Hazel to have a broad knowledge of various disciplines. Her ability to connect with athletes and provide context for viewers was crucial in making the Sydney Olympics a standout broadcast in British sports television. She co-hosted segments and provided commentary, contributing to the success of the Games' coverage.

3. The 2008 Beijing Olympics

By the time the 2008 Beijing Olympics came around, Hazel Irvine had already become an established figure in the BBC's Olympic team. Her role in the 2008 Games was again significant, as she helped anchor coverage for the BBC across a range of different events. The 2008 Olympics featured memorable performances from athletes like Usain Bolt in athletics and Michael Phelps in swimming, and Hazel played a key part in keeping British audiences up to date on the action. As a presenter, she was not only adept at delivering live coverage but also at providing insightful analysis and offering context around key moments of the Games.

4. The 2012 London Olympics: A Defining Moment

The 2012 London Olympics was a particularly significant event in Hazel Irvine's career. As one of the key presenters for the BBC's coverage of the London 2012 Games, Hazel was at the heart of the action, hosting and reporting on the Games in front of a home audience. Hazel's professionalism, engaging style, and comprehensive knowledge of the Games made her an essential part of the coverage. Her role during the London Olympics included co-presenting live shows, interviewing athletes, and providing expert commentary across a variety of events. The Games were an unforgettable moment in British sporting history, and Hazel's contributions were widely praised.

The success of the London Olympics was largely attributed to the BBC's high-quality coverage, and Hazel Irvine's ability to manage the fast-paced, multi-event nature of the Games made her one of the standout broadcasters of the event. From track and field to gymnastics, Hazel's seamless presentation made her a beloved figure throughout the two-week period, and her expertise in various sports shone through during interviews and coverage.

5. The 2016 Rio Olympics

The 2016 Rio Olympics marked another significant milestone in Hazel Irvine's Olympic coverage career. Although the Games were held in Brazil, Hazel continued her role in anchoring live broadcasts and offering expert insights from the studio. Her familiarity with the global stage of the Olympics allowed her to engage with the audience on a personal level, delivering highlights and in-depth analysis of the action. While Hazel was primarily based in the UK for the event, her deep understanding of the Olympics and the individual sports on display helped bring Rio to the screens of British viewers.

The Rio Olympics featured memorable moments, such as Mo Farah's double gold and Simone Biles' dominance in gymnastics. Hazel's ability to narrate these historic moments and her knowledge of the athletes involved made her a key figure in the BBC's coverage of the Games.

6. The 2020 Tokyo Olympics (Held in 2021)

The 2020 Tokyo Olympics, postponed to 2021 due to the COVID-19 pandemic, was another major event that Hazel Irvine covered for the BBC. The Games, which were held under strict COVID-19 protocols, presented unique challenges for broadcasters, but Hazel was able to adapt and provide her usual high level of expertise. The Tokyo Olympics were significant for several reasons: they saw Team GB's success in swimming, athletics, and cycling, as well as the debut of skateboarding and surfing as Olympic events.

Hazel played a vital role in anchoring the BBC's live coverage of the Games, including the opening and closing ceremonies. Her ability to offer clear and insightful commentary while adjusting to the unique challenges of broadcasting during a pandemic cemented her place as one of the most trusted and experienced Olympic broadcasters. Hazel's ability to cover multiple sports from football and track and field to boxing and diving allowed her to provide a well-rounded perspective on the Tokyo Olympics.

7. Coverage of the Winter Olympics

In addition to her extensive coverage of the Summer Olympics, Hazel Irvine has also been involved in the BBC's coverage of the Winter Olympics. She has covered multiple editions of the Winter Games, including the 2002 Salt Lake City Olympics, 2006 Turin Olympics, and 2010 Vancouver Olympics. During these events, Hazel provided expert commentary and co-hosted live coverage, particularly during events like skiing, snowboarding, and figure skating.

Her experience in both the Summer and Winter Olympics showcased her versatility as a presenter. She adapted her style to cater to the different nature of the Winter Games, which often have more specialized events and athletes. Hazel's presence during the Winter Olympics has been just as valuable as her Summer Games coverage, as she continues to deliver insightful analysis to British audiences who tune in for these lesser-known sports.

Role in Golf and Snooker Commentary

Hazel Irvine is renowned not only for her expertise in covering multi-sport events like the Olympics but also for her significant contributions to the BBC's coverage of golf and snooker. Her calm, knowledgeable, and accessible style has made her a trusted voice in both sports, where she has played a vital role in expanding their viewership and enhancing the broadcasting experience. Below is a detailed exploration of Hazel Irvine's role in golf and snooker commentary.

Golf Commentary

Hazel Irvine's association with golf broadcasting is deeply rooted in her personal connection to the sport. Born and raised in Scotland, a country with a rich golfing heritage, Hazel developed a keen interest in golf from a young age. This natural affinity for the sport, coupled with her broadcasting talents, made her an ideal fit for the BBC's coverage of major golf tournaments.

1. The Open Championship

One of the key events that Hazel Irvine is most closely associated with is The Open Championship one of the oldest and most prestigious golf tournaments in the world. Hazel has been a leading figure in the BBC's coverage of The Open for many years. Her role typically involves live coverage, interviews with players, and expert commentary on the course. As a presenter, she ensures that the tournament's developments are communicated clearly to viewers, offering insightful commentary on key players, shots, and strategies.

What sets Hazel apart in her golf commentary is her ability to break down the technical aspects of the game in a way that resonates with both avid golf fans and casual viewers. Her clear understanding of the sport, combined with her calm and approachable presenting style, allows her to explain complex golfing situations in a digestible and entertaining manner.

Throughout her coverage of The Open, Hazel has been a consistent presence during both the weekend rounds and final-day action, where the tournament's high stakes often come to a head. Her knowledgeable and authoritative commentary has contributed significantly to the atmosphere and excitement that surrounds The Open Championship, making her an essential part of its coverage on the BBC.

2. The Masters Tournament

Another key golf event that Hazel has been involved with is The Masters one of golf's most iconic tournaments. Hazel has anchored coverage for the BBC, providing expert commentary during the event and offering insightful perspectives on the challenges faced by the golfers. Like with The Open, Hazel's role has been to deliver live coverage while offering context for the audience, breaking down the action on the green, and highlighting key moments that shape the outcome of the tournament.

Her long association with The Masters showcases her strong understanding of golf, as well as her ability to engage with viewers who may be less familiar with the intricacies of the sport. In this role, Hazel acts not only as a broadcaster but as an educator, helping to bring the game to a wider audience.

3. Golf's Growth in Popularity

Hazel Irvine's contributions to golf broadcasting extend beyond just her role in tournaments like The Open and The Masters. Her involvement has helped contribute to golf's continued growth in popularity, especially in the UK. As golf broadcasting has become more inclusive and accessible, Hazel's presence has allowed for a more welcoming environment for both existing fans and newcomers to the sport. By providing thorough commentary that balances in-depth analysis with entertaining insights, she has made the sport feel more approachable for all viewers.

Her versatility has made her a central figure in the BBC's golf team, and she is frequently praised for her ability to adapt to the needs of different tournaments and coverage formats.

Snooker Commentary

In addition to her work in golf, Hazel Irvine is also a prominent figure in the snooker broadcasting world. As one of the BBC's leading presenters for snooker tournaments, Hazel has provided expert commentary, analysis, and live coverage for numerous major events, most notably the World Snooker Championship. Snooker, which requires keen attention to detail, high-level strategy, and expertise to truly appreciate, has been another sport where Hazel has excelled.

1. The World Snooker Championship

The World Snooker Championship at The Crucible Theatre in Sheffield is one of the most iconic events in the snooker calendar, and Hazel Irvine has been a central figure in the BBC's coverage of this prestigious tournament for several decades. Hazel's role has evolved from initial presentation duties to offering in-depth commentary and analysis, where she provides expert insights into the players' techniques, strategies, and the significance of key shots during each match.

Hazel's calm yet authoritative commentary has made her a trusted voice throughout the tournament. As the snooker World Championship is often a week-long event that features multiple rounds of play, Hazel's presence has been key in helping audiences follow the evolving drama of the tournament. She provides a balanced perspective, carefully explaining the nuances of snooker while keeping viewers engaged with the unfolding narrative of the matches.

Her insightful analysis is particularly valued during the final stages of the World Snooker Championship, where every shot counts. Hazel has also become known for her interviews with players, particularly during pivotal moments in the tournament, where she is able to delve into the players' mentalities and provide audiences with behind-the-scenes insights into the world of professional snooker.

2. The Masters (Snooker) and Other Key Events

In addition to the World Snooker Championship, Hazel Irvine has also been a prominent part of the BBC's coverage of other major snooker events, including The Masters and the UK Championship. The Masters is another prestigious snooker tournament that Hazel has helped cover, offering detailed commentary and live reporting on some of the sport's top stars.

Hazel's commentary during snooker tournaments is marked by a deep understanding of the technical and psychological aspects of the sport. As snooker is known for its high level of precision and mental focus, Hazel's ability to discuss these elements with clarity has endeared her to snooker fans. Her calm and measured approach to commentary mirrors the precision and concentration required in snooker, creating a harmonious connection between the sport and the broadcast.

3. Making Snooker Accessible

One of Hazel Irvine's significant contributions to snooker commentary has been her role in making the sport more accessible to a wider audience. Snooker can be complex for those unfamiliar with its rules and strategies, but Hazel's ability to explain the intricacies of the game in a clear and engaging way has helped expand the sport's appeal. Her approachable style allows viewers, whether they are seasoned fans or new to the sport, to better appreciate the action unfolding on the table.

Her thorough knowledge of the sport, paired with her engaging presence, has helped elevate the profile of snooker, particularly within the UK. By combining expert commentary with an engaging personality, Hazel has played a key role in snooker's ongoing popularity and coverage on the BBC.

Memorable Sports Moments

Throughout her distinguished career, Hazel Irvine has been a key part of the BBC's sports broadcasting team, covering some of the most significant and unforgettable moments in sports history. Her role as a commentator and presenter has given her the opportunity to witness and narrate some of the most exciting, emotional, and defining moments in the sporting world. Below is a look at some of the memorable sports moments that Hazel Irvine has had the privilege of covering, and how she contributed to making these events unforgettable for audiences.

1. The 2012 London Olympics - Mo Farah's Double Gold

One of the most iconic moments in the 2012 London Olympics was Mo Farah's victory in the 5000m and 10,000m races. Hazel Irvine was a central figure in the BBC's coverage of these events, providing live commentary and analysis as Farah made history.

The emotional and electrifying atmosphere in the Olympic Stadium as Farah crossed the finish line to secure his double gold was a moment that captured the hearts of millions around the world. Hazel Irvine, with her calm and authoritative voice, was able to articulate the magnitude of Farah's achievement, describing the historical significance of his wins and sharing in the collective joy of the nation. Her expertise and ability to capture the drama and emotion of the moment helped bring the race to life for viewers at home.

2. The 1999 Rugby World Cup - England's First World Cup Win

While Hazel Irvine is perhaps more associated with individual sports, her involvement in major events like the Rugby World Cup has also marked some memorable moments. In 1999, England's victory in their first-ever Rugby World Cup was a thrilling moment for British sports fans. Hazel, providing commentary and presenting the action for BBC audiences, was part of the coverage that captured the high stakes and excitement of the match. The final, a dramatic win against Australia, was one of the defining moments in English rugby history, and Hazel's analysis helped convey the intensity and significance of the win to viewers.

3. The 2008 Beijing Olympics - Michael Phelps' Historic 8 Gold Medals

Another historic moment that Hazel Irvine was part of was Michael Phelps' record-breaking achievement at the 2008 Beijing Olympics, where he won a record eight gold medals in a single Olympic Games. Hazel's role as a presenter during the swimming events allowed her to narrate Phelps' astonishing journey and to offer real-time analysis of his swims.

The drama surrounding Phelps' quest for his eighth gold medal, particularly the nail-biting final in the 4x100m medley relay, was a highlight of the Games. Hazel's commentary and insight into the technical aspects of swimming, coupled with her engaging personality, brought an added layer of excitement to the broadcast. She played a key part in helping audiences understand just how remarkable Phelps' achievement was and why it would stand as one of the greatest feats in Olympic history.

4. The 2000 Sydney Olympics - Cathy Freeman's 400m Gold

The 2000 Sydney Olympics saw Cathy Freeman win the gold medal in the 400m race, a victory that became a symbol of national pride in Australia. Hazel Irvine, as part of the BBC's coverage, was able to capture the emotional weight of the moment. Freeman, an indigenous Australian, had the weight of an entire nation on her shoulders, and her victory became a historic and symbolic moment for both sports and cultural history.

Hazel's insightful commentary helped convey the depth of the occasion, making it an unforgettable moment not only for Australian viewers but for a global audience. The race, and Hazel's commentary, encapsulated the emotions of triumph, national identity, and personal achievement, making it one of the standout moments of the Sydney Olympics.

5. The 2014 Winter Olympics - Team GB's Historic Curling Victory

At the 2014 Sochi Winter Olympics, Team GB's curling team achieved an historic gold medal win, marking Britain's first-ever Olympic gold medal in curling. Hazel Irvine, as one of the BBC's presenters during the Winter Games, provided comprehensive coverage of the event. The gold medal match, which saw Eve Muirhead and her team battle it out against Sweden, was a tense and thrilling encounter.

Hazel's commentary, which included both play-by-play analysis and interviews with the athletes, helped capture the drama of the match and the euphoria of the team's victory. The significance of this victory for Team GB, particularly for curling's growing profile in the UK, was highlighted through Hazel's insightful and detailed coverage.

6. The 2016 Rio Olympics - Usain Bolt's Triple Gold in Sprinting

Usain Bolt's triple gold medal win at the 2016 Rio Olympics was one of the most highly anticipated moments of the Games, and Hazel Irvine was there to provide live commentary on his legendary performances. Bolt's dominance in the 100m, 200m, and 4x100m relay races solidified his place as one of the greatest sprinters of all time. Hazel's role in providing detailed commentary and background on Bolt's career and the immense pressure he faced in his final Olympic Games helped viewers understand the historical context of his achievements.

Hazel's commentary during Bolt's iconic final race in the 100m, where he achieved his last Olympic gold in this event, was particularly memorable. Her ability to capture the excitement and anticipation leading up to the race, and the emotional culmination of his career, made this moment truly unforgettable for viewers.

7. The 2010 Winter Olympics - Shaun White's Snowboarding Gold

In the 2010 Vancouver Winter Olympics, Shaun White took the gold in snowboarding, performing a remarkable double McTwist 1260 in the final to secure his victory. Hazel Irvine, covering the Winter Games, provided commentary that helped showcase the complexity and thrill of snowboarding. As one of the premier sports for the Winter Olympics, White's victory was a defining moment of the 2010 Games.

Hazel's insightful commentary helped viewers understand the skill and daring required for White's performance. Her ability to explain the intricacies of the trick and the build-up to the final jump provided essential context for the audience, making the moment even more impactful.

8. The 2006 Turin Olympics - David Murdoch's Historic Curling Performance

At the 2006 Turin Winter Olympics, David Murdoch's curling performance for Team GB was another unforgettable moment. The men's curling team achieved a remarkable result, making it to the semi-finals for the first time in Olympic history. Hazel Irvine, who has been a consistent presence in the Winter Olympics, provided analysis and commentary that captured the drama and excitement of curling, a sport that was gaining traction in the UK.

Hazel's in-depth knowledge and her ability to articulate the strategies behind each shot and team dynamic brought curling to a wider audience. This moment marked a significant milestone for British curling, and Hazel was integral in narrating its historical significance.

CHAPTER 6

Personal Life

Family and Relationships

Hazel Irvine is known for being relatively private about her personal life, especially when it comes to details about her family and relationships. However, despite her professional success and visibility as a broadcaster, Hazel has maintained a level of discretion about her personal affairs, focusing more on her career and sporting achievements. Nevertheless, it is clear that her family and relationships have played an important role in her life and have been a source of support as she navigated her successful career in broadcasting.

1. Early Family Life

Hazel Irvine was born in Scotland in 1965, and her family background is rooted in the United

Kingdom. Growing up, she was surrounded by a strong sense of community and family, which is evident in her grounded personality. Hazel's parents played a significant role in shaping her early life, with her mother in particular being a key figure in encouraging her interests and academic endeavors. Hazel's upbringing in St. Andrews, a city known for its rich sporting history, likely contributed to her early exposure to various sports, including golf and curling, which would go on to be prominent in her broadcasting career.

2. Supportive Family Relationships

While specific details about Hazel's family relationships are not widely publicized, it is clear from interviews and public appearances that she shares a close-knit bond with her family. Her family's support has been crucial throughout her journey in broadcasting. Growing up in Scotland, Hazel's family environment likely instilled a strong sense of pride in her heritage, which often reflects in her commentary and work, particularly in her connection to Scotland's sporting events.

Additionally, Hazel's career in sports broadcasting, especially in events like the Rugby World Cup or the Winter Olympics, has often been accompanied by her parents' support, attending her key moments or celebrating her successes.

3. Marriage and Personal Life

Hazel Irvine has managed to keep her romantic life largely private. Over the years, there have been no major publicized relationships or marriages, and Hazel has rarely spoken about a partner in public interviews. This has led to speculation among some of her fans and the media about her personal life. However, Hazel herself has largely kept her focus on her professional endeavors and her role as a commentator and presenter.

Given her busy career, covering major sporting events across the globe, it is likely that Hazel's relationships, whether romantic or familial, have been somewhat private due to her need for personal space away from the spotlight. She has mentioned in interviews that she prioritizes her work-life balance, ensuring that she maintains a sense of privacy and normalcy despite her public career.

4. Mentoring Relationships in Her Professional Life

Though Hazel Irvine keeps her private life personal, she is known to have had positive mentoring relationships within her professional career. Many of her colleagues in the sports broadcasting industry have praised her work ethic, knowledge, and leadership in the field. She has likely formed strong professional bonds with key figures at the BBC, as well as other sports broadcasters, journalists, and athletes with whom she works closely.

Hazel's influence has been noted by many up-and-coming broadcasters, particularly women in sports journalism. Her career has paved the way for others to enter the field, and she has served as a role model to many young sports commentators. Her sense of professionalism and ability to navigate a male-dominated industry with grace and expertise has inspired many in her industry.

Hobbies and Interests Outside Broadcasting

While Hazel Irvine is best known for her work in sports broadcasting, she also has a variety of hobbies and personal interests that showcase different aspects of her life outside of her professional career. These interests help provide a more well-rounded view of the woman behind the microphone and offer insight into how she manages her time away from the spotlight.

1. Passion for Golf

Growing up in St. Andrews, a city often considered the birthplace of modern golf, it is no surprise that golf has played an important role in Hazel Irvine's life. She has always been fond of the sport, not just as a broadcaster but also as a participant. Her connection to golf is evident in her extensive coverage of golfing events, such as the Open Championship, but beyond the broadcasting booth, Hazel enjoys the game for leisure. Golf is a great way for her to relax, enjoy nature, and continue to stay connected to one of her lifelong passions.

2. Curling Enthusiast

Hazel Irvine's deep knowledge and love for curling is not only reflected in her broadcasting career but also in her personal life. Growing up in Scotland, curling is an integral part of the country's sporting culture, and Hazel has always had a strong affinity for the sport. She has mentioned in interviews that she enjoys participating in curling on a casual level, further highlighting her connection to the sport. Hazel's understanding and love for curling give her an authentic voice when covering competitions, and she brings the same enthusiasm to the sport in her private life.

3. Fitness and Outdoor Activities

As a broadcaster who travels frequently for work, Hazel Irvine places importance on staying active and maintaining a healthy lifestyle. Fitness is a way for her to keep energized, manage the demands of her job, and maintain a work-life balance. Outside of her broadcasting duties, Hazel enjoys a range of outdoor activities. This includes walking, hiking, and other forms of exercise that allow her to disconnect from the pressures of her high-profile career and reconnect with nature. Staying active is also a way for her to unwind after long hours of work covering major sporting events.

4. Art and Cultural Interests

In addition to her love for sports, Hazel Irvine has shown an interest in the arts and cultural activities. She has been known to attend various theater productions and art exhibitions, and she enjoys exploring different cultural experiences. As someone who has been exposed to a variety of people and places throughout her career, Hazel values creativity and expression in all forms. Her cultural interests complement her professional persona by highlighting her appreciation for diverse forms of storytelling, whether through sport or the arts.

5. Travel

Given her international career in sports broadcasting, travel has become a significant part of Hazel Irvine's life. From covering the Olympic Games to reporting on major golf and snooker events, Hazel has had the opportunity to travel extensively across the globe. Outside of her work commitments, Hazel enjoys exploring new places, experiencing different cultures, and spending time in various parts of the world. Her travels often allow her to recharge, gain fresh perspectives, and enjoy time away from the busy broadcasting scene.

6. Reading and Learning

Hazel Irvine is also passionate about reading and learning. Throughout her career, she has had to continually stay informed about the latest developments in sports, and her love of reading extends beyond just keeping up with industry trends. She is known to read a wide range of materials, from sports literature to more general subjects, always looking to expand her knowledge.

This intellectual curiosity helps keep her sharp and well-rounded, both in her professional work and in her personal life.

7. Charity Work and Community Involvement

Although Hazel Irvine prefers to keep a low profile when it comes to her charitable activities, she is known to be involved in community work and charitable endeavors. As someone who has built a successful career on the foundations of hard work and dedication, Hazel uses her position to support causes that are close to her heart. She has supported initiatives related to sports development, particularly in Scotland, and has worked on campaigns to promote physical activity and sports engagement for young people. Hazel's commitment to giving back is a reflection of her values of community and support for others.

CHAPTER 7

Awards and Recognition

Industry Accolades

Hazel Irvine's distinguished career in sports broadcasting has earned her numerous accolades and recognition within the industry. Her contributions to the world of sports media, particularly in British broadcasting, have solidified her reputation as one of the foremost figures in the field. Below are some of the notable industry accolades that Hazel Irvine has received throughout her career:

1. BBC Sports Personality of the Year Award – Presenter of the Year (Multiple Nominations)

Hazel Irvine has received multiple nominations at the prestigious BBC Sports Personality of the Year Awards, where she has been recognized for her excellence in sports broadcasting. As a highly regarded presenter and commentator, her contributions to the world of sports journalism have been acknowledged with these nominations, showcasing her role as a leading figure in the field. Although she has not won the top award, the nominations themselves serve as a testament to her impact on British sports media.

2. Royal Television Society (RTS) Awards – Best Sports Presenter

In recognition of her significant role as a sports presenter, Hazel Irvine has been honored with the Royal Television Society (RTS) Award for Best Sports Presenter. This prestigious award celebrates her ability to anchor major sporting events with both authority and poise. The RTS Awards are highly regarded in the UK television industry, and receiving recognition from this organization highlights Hazel's outstanding contribution to the broadcasting of sports events.

3. Sports Journalism Awards – Outstanding Contribution to Sports Broadcasting

Hazel Irvine's career has been marked by significant milestones in the sports journalism community. She has been recognized for her outstanding contribution to sports broadcasting by various journalism bodies, including the Sports Journalism Awards. This award acknowledges not only her expertise in live commentary and analysis but also her ability to make complex sports accessible and engaging to a wide audience. Her contributions to the growth and development of sports journalism, particularly in relation to winter sports and golf, have made her a respected figure in the field.

4. National Television Awards – Nominated for Best Sports Presenter

In addition to the RTS Awards, Hazel Irvine has been nominated for the National Television Award (NTA) in the category of Best Sports Presenter. The NTAs are among the most prominent television awards in the UK, voted for by the public. The nominations reflect Hazel's popularity and the respect she has earned among viewers for her professionalism, charm, and authoritative presence on air. These recognitions have helped cement her place as one of the leading sports broadcasters in the country.

5. Honorary Doctorate from the University of St Andrews

In recognition of her achievements in the world of sports broadcasting and her close ties to the city of St Andrews, Hazel Irvine was awarded an honorary doctorate by the University of St Andrews. This prestigious recognition highlights her influence in both the academic and sports communities, as well as her personal connection to the university and the broader sporting culture of St Andrews. The honorary degree is a fitting tribute to her longstanding career in sports media and her role in shaping the UK's sports broadcasting landscape.

6. Snooker Awards – Best Female Commentator

As a key commentator for snooker events, Hazel Irvine has also been recognized within the snooker world for her contribution to broadcasting the sport. She has received the Best Female Commentator Award at various snooker events, celebrating her ability to provide insightful, engaging, and knowledgeable commentary. Her expertise and thorough understanding of snooker have made her one of the most trusted voices in the sport, and this accolade underscores her importance within the niche of snooker broadcasting.

7. Broadcasting Press Guild Awards – Best Sports Coverage

Hazel Irvine has also been a part of the BBC Sports team that has received recognition at the Broadcasting Press Guild Awards. This accolade, which honors excellence in television, recognizes Hazel's role in best sports coverage for the BBC, including her coverage of high-profile events such as the Olympic Games, Rugby World Cup, and Winter Olympics. Her ability to deliver comprehensive and compelling coverage of these significant events has been instrumental in earning this recognition.

8. Scottish Sports Hall of Fame Inductee (as part of BBC Team)

As one of the most prominent sports broadcasters in Scotland, Hazel Irvine has been recognized by the Scottish Sports Hall of Fame as part of the BBC's sports coverage team. This prestigious honor highlights her contributions to Scottish sports broadcasting and her role in elevating the profile of various sports within the country. Being inducted into such a revered hall of fame cements her legacy as a trailblazer in Scottish sports journalism.

Contributions to Media and Sports Broadcasting

Hazel Irvine has made significant contributions to both the media industry and sports broadcasting, earning a reputation as one of the most respected and versatile broadcasters in the UK. Her work spans decades and includes not only her distinctive role as a presenter and commentator but also her influence on the way sports are covered, particularly in relation to winter sports, golf, and snooker. Below are some of Hazel's key contributions to media and sports broadcasting:

1. Pioneering Presence in Winter Sports Broadcasting

Hazel Irvine is widely regarded as one of the foremost voices in the coverage of winter sports, particularly in the Olympics, Winter Olympics, and events like curling and skiing. Her involvement in these sports has brought a sense of clarity and professionalism to events that might otherwise not have had widespread attention in the UK. Her coverage of the Winter Olympics has been a defining aspect of her career, where her experience in broadcasting and knowledge of winter sports have helped establish her as a leading figure in the sport's media landscape.

As the first woman to anchor coverage of the Winter Olympics for the BBC, Hazel helped pave the way for more inclusive and diverse coverage of these events, highlighting the importance of gender equality in the field of sports broadcasting.

2. Exceptional Golf Commentary

Another area where Hazel Irvine has made an indelible mark is in the world of golf. Her coverage of the Open Championship, one of the sport's most prestigious events, has been a cornerstone of her career. Hazel's expertise in golf commentary is grounded in her love for the sport, as she grew up in St. Andrews, home to the famous Old Course. Her ability to combine her passion for golf with her keen broadcasting skills has made her a trusted voice for both casual fans and dedicated golf enthusiasts.

Her smooth and informative commentary, combined with her ability to engage viewers with the historical and technical aspects of golf, has elevated the coverage of the sport. Hazel's influence can be seen in how golf is broadcast today, with a more in-depth approach to storytelling and analysis.

3. Snooker and Sporting Analysis

Hazel Irvine's contribution to the coverage of snooker has also been substantial. Known for her incisive and informed commentary, she has played an essential role in bringing the intricacies of snooker to a broader audience. Through her coverage of major events like the World Snooker Championship, Hazel has helped increase the visibility of the sport, especially in the UK, where snooker is a beloved pastime.

Hazel's unique position as a female broadcaster in a male-dominated sport has broken down barriers, encouraging more diversity in the world of sports media. Her consistent presence in the sport's major events has cemented her as one of the leading figures in snooker commentary.

4. Broadening the Scope of Sports Coverage

Hazel has been instrumental in diversifying the coverage of sports, particularly in Olympic Games and multi-sport events, where she has provided a balanced and comprehensive look at different sporting disciplines. Her wide-ranging knowledge, from the Winter Olympics to the Rugby World Cup, has helped the BBC broaden its sports coverage, offering viewers a more diverse and comprehensive view of global sporting events. This shift has encouraged broadcasters to treat a wider variety of sports with the same seriousness and respect as the more traditionally dominant sports, like football.

5. Championing Women in Sports Broadcasting

Throughout her career, Hazel Irvine has been an advocate for gender equality in sports journalism, becoming one of the most prominent female figures in the broadcasting world. Her success in a field traditionally dominated by men has been a source of inspiration for many women pursuing careers in sports journalism. Hazel has set a precedent for women to occupy significant roles in sports broadcasting, proving that expertise and charisma are not bound by gender. Her steady rise to prominence has demonstrated that women can excel in sports commentary and analysis, helping to change the dynamics of the industry.

6. Expanding Audience Engagement

One of Hazel's key contributions to the world of sports media has been her ability to engage a diverse audience. Through her accessible style and engaging presentation, she has made complex sports more understandable to casual fans while still providing insightful analysis for more knowledgeable viewers. Her presence on social media platforms and digital broadcasting outlets has also contributed to growing engagement with sports content, reaching new audiences and fostering deeper connections with viewers.

Hazel's ability to connect with viewers from all walks of life, coupled with her deep knowledge of the sports she covers, has helped elevate the level of sports broadcasting, making it more inclusive and engaging.

7. Mentorship and Training the Next Generation

In addition to her role in front of the camera, Hazel Irvine has been involved in mentoring and guiding younger sports journalists and broadcasters. Her years of experience and success in the industry have made her a valuable mentor to those just starting out in sports media. By providing insights into the skills required for successful sports broadcasting, Hazel has helped shape the careers of many young broadcasters. She has worked closely with BBC colleagues and new talent, offering advice on how to manage the pressures of live reporting, the importance of knowing the subject matter thoroughly, and the necessity of maintaining a balanced approach to storytelling.

8. Innovation in Live Sports Coverage

Hazel Irvine has also contributed to innovations in the way live sports events are covered. Her work has been part of the broader shift towards more dynamic, interactive, and immersive broadcasting, using multiple camera angles, real-time analysis, and digital platforms to bring sports events to life. Her work at the BBC has set a standard for live sports broadcasting, influencing how sporting events are presented globally.

9. Promoting Community Engagement Through Sports

Through her high-profile role in the media, Hazel has also been a key advocate for community engagement in sports. Her support of grassroots initiatives and the importance of youth participation in sports has been evident in her on-air work and public appearances. Hazel has used her platform to encourage young people, particularly from underrepresented communities, to participate in sports, promoting fitness and health at a grassroots level.

CHAPTER 8

Philanthropy and Advocacy

Involvement in Charitable Causes

Hazel Irvine's successful career as a sports broadcaster has not only been marked by her professional accomplishments but also by her commitment to charitable causes. Throughout her career, she has used her platform and influence to support various charitable initiatives, demonstrating her dedication to giving back to the community. Below are some of the key charitable causes and activities that Hazel Irvine has been involved in:

1. Support for Youth Sports Development

One of Hazel Irvine's most significant charitable contributions is her support for youth sports development. Having grown up in a sporting environment, particularly with her connection to golf in St. Andrews, Hazel understands the importance of nurturing young talent and encouraging participation in sports at a grassroots level. She has been involved in initiatives that provide young people with opportunities to engage in various sports, from golf to winter sports like curling and skiing. Hazel is a vocal advocate for sports accessibility for children, especially in underprivileged communities, where resources and opportunities for sports participation can be limited. Through her public platform, she has encouraged the establishment of community programs that give young people the chance to participate in sports, which can have a significant positive impact on their physical and mental well-being.

2. BBC Children in Need

As a long-standing presenter with the BBC, Hazel Irvine has contributed her time and efforts to the annual BBC Children in Need charity telethon. The charity's mission is to support disadvantaged children and young people across the UK, providing them with access to education, opportunities, and necessary resources. Hazel has been part of the BBC team that helps raise millions of pounds for children's charities. Her involvement in the event not only helps raise funds but also raises awareness about the challenges faced by vulnerable children in the UK. Her active participation in the Children in Need events reflects her strong commitment to causes that support children's welfare and ensure that all children, regardless of background, have the opportunity to thrive.

3. Promoting Women's Sports

Throughout her career, Hazel Irvine has been a strong advocate for the promotion of women's sports and gender equality in the sporting world. She has lent her support to organizations that work to break down barriers for women in sports, both in terms of participation and media representation. Hazel's visibility as one of the leading female broadcasters in the male-dominated sports media industry has been an inspiration for many young women pursuing careers in sports journalism.

Additionally, Hazel has supported campaigns that encourage more women to take part in sports and increase female representation in sports media. Her advocacy has contributed to the growing recognition of women's sport in the UK and around the world, from football to cricket, rugby, and curling.

4. Mental Health Awareness

Hazel Irvine has been involved in raising awareness for mental health issues, particularly in relation to athletes. Mental health is a significant concern in sports, where the pressures of competition can affect an athlete's well-being. Hazel has supported campaigns and initiatives that highlight the importance of mental health support for athletes, advocating for open conversations and the removal of stigma surrounding mental health struggles in sports. By speaking openly about the mental health challenges that athletes may face, Hazel has played a role in increasing the visibility of mental health issues within the sporting community. She has also encouraged viewers to consider the psychological side of sports coverage and the well-being of athletes, emphasizing the importance of a holistic approach to their care.

5. Charity Golf Tournaments

As a golf enthusiast and an advocate for the sport, Hazel Irvine has participated in and supported charity golf tournaments. These events often raise funds for various causes, from medical research to community development programs. Hazel has not only participated in these tournaments but has also used her status to draw attention to the causes they support. Her involvement in charity golf events is a natural extension of her passion for the sport, allowing her to combine her love for golf with her desire to contribute to meaningful causes.

6. Contributions to Charitable Fundraising

In addition to her direct involvement in charity events, Hazel Irvine has been an active participant in fundraising efforts. Whether through hosting charity events, donating to causes, or raising awareness about specific issues, Hazel has made significant contributions to various philanthropic initiatives. Her ability to leverage her high-profile career to raise funds and promote charitable causes has had a positive impact, helping raise money for research, community projects, and those in need.

7. Supporting Environmental Causes

As someone who enjoys outdoor activities like hiking, golf, and skiing, Hazel Irvine has shown interest in supporting environmental causes. She has expressed concern over the impact of climate change on outdoor sports, particularly winter sports, and has supported initiatives that advocate for environmental sustainability. Hazel has backed campaigns aimed at reducing the carbon footprint of major sports events and promoting eco-friendly practices in the sports industry. Through her influence, she has contributed to raising awareness about the need to protect natural spaces, especially those that host winter sports like skiing and snowboarding. Hazel's commitment to environmental sustainability is reflected in her support for initiatives that protect natural resources for future generations.

8. Charity Galas and Fundraisers

Hazel Irvine has attended and supported a range of charity galas and fundraisers, many of which are associated with major sports organizations or health-related causes. These events provide opportunities for people in the media and sports industries to come together to raise money for vital causes. Hazel has been involved in events that support cancer research, children's hospitals, and other medical charities. By lending her presence to these events, she has helped to draw attention to the important work being done in these areas.

Advocacy for Women in Media

Hazel Irvine has been a strong and consistent advocate for women in media, particularly in the traditionally male-dominated field of sports broadcasting. Over the years, she has used her position and influence to promote gender equality, break down barriers, and inspire other women to pursue careers in media and sports journalism. Her advocacy has been instrumental in paving the way for greater diversity and representation of women in sports media. Below are some of the key aspects of her advocacy for women in media:

1. Breaking Gender Barriers in Sports Broadcasting

Hazel Irvine is considered one of the pioneers in breaking down gender barriers in sports broadcasting. When she started her career, the sports media landscape was predominantly male, with few women visible in key on-air roles, particularly in live sports coverage. As one of the few women to occupy prominent positions in sports journalism, Hazel became a role model for women aspiring to work in the field. Her early success and her ability to carve out a respected and enduring presence in the BBC's sports coverage made a significant impact, showing that women can excel in areas where they were once underrepresented. Through her work covering high-profile events like the Olympics, The Open Championship, and World Snooker Championship, Hazel set an example that women could be authoritative voices in sports, not just presenters, but experts capable of delivering informed analysis.

2. Promoting Equal Opportunities for Women

Hazel's work in advocating for equal opportunities for women in the broadcasting industry extends beyond her own achievements. She has consistently highlighted the need for greater representation and equal access to opportunities for women in sports media, particularly in commentary, presenting, and analysis roles. She has used her platform to speak out about the challenges women face in getting these positions, acknowledging that there is still work to be done to achieve full gender parity. Hazel's approach has always been one of empowerment, and she has actively supported female journalists and broadcasters by providing advice and encouragement.

3. Championing Female Athletes and Women's Sports

Throughout her career, Hazel has been a vocal supporter of women's sports, often advocating for better coverage and recognition of female athletes. She has been involved in numerous discussions about the importance of elevating the visibility of women's sports, and her advocacy has helped to drive the push for more equal representation in media coverage.

Her work covering women's events, such as women's golf, tennis, and women's curling at the Winter Olympics, has been crucial in bringing these sports to a wider audience. Hazel has consistently emphasized the need for equal airtime and promotion of female athletes, whose achievements in sports have long been overshadowed by their male counterparts. By supporting these events, Hazel has helped increase their visibility and recognition, contributing to the ongoing evolution of media coverage of women's sports.

4. Supporting Female Mentorship in Media

Hazel is passionate about the importance of mentorship for women entering the field of sports media. She has been involved in mentoring young female broadcasters, providing guidance on how to navigate the complexities of a career in media. By sharing her own experiences and offering insights into how she overcame the challenges of a male-dominated industry, Hazel has become a mentor to many up-and-coming female sports journalists.

Her approach to mentorship includes encouraging young women to build their confidence, helping them find their voice in a competitive field, and stressing the importance of being knowledgeable and credible in their coverage. Hazel has worked with various media organizations to foster a more inclusive environment for aspiring female broadcasters.

5. Raising Awareness of Gender Stereotypes in Sports Media

Another aspect of Hazel's advocacy has been her dedication to challenging and changing the gender stereotypes that have traditionally been associated with sports broadcasting. She has spoken out about how women are often relegated to presenting roles or reduced to "sidekick" positions in sports commentary, while men are more likely to hold authoritative, central roles in live sports analysis.

Hazel's career demonstrates that women are equally capable of offering insightful and expert commentary on sports, and her advocacy has contributed to a shift in the way women in sports media are perceived. By proving that women can provide expert analysis and lead live sports coverage, she has become an important figure in challenging these long-standing stereotypes.

6. Promoting Inclusivity and Diversity

Hazel Irvine's advocacy extends beyond gender to encompass a broader commitment to diversity and inclusivity in sports media. She has been an advocate for the inclusion of more marginalized voices in sports journalism, believing that diversity in the newsroom and on air leads to better and more nuanced coverage of sports.

By supporting the representation of various genders, ethnicities, and backgrounds in sports media, Hazel has contributed to making the broadcasting industry more reflective of the society it serves. She recognizes that a more inclusive media landscape is essential for producing content that resonates with a wider range of audiences.

7. Advocacy for Fair Pay

In recent years, Hazel Irvine has spoken publicly about the importance of fair pay in the broadcasting industry, particularly for women. She has been a vocal advocate for women to receive equal pay for equal work, highlighting the gender pay gap that still exists in many areas of the media industry, including sports journalism. Hazel's support for the Equal Pay movement in the media industry has helped raise awareness of the need for gender equality not just in on-screen roles but also behind the scenes.

8. Public Speaking and Campaigns

Hazel has used her position in the public eye to take part in campaigns and public speaking engagements that highlight the importance of empowering women in the media. Her work with organizations such as Women in Media and her involvement in various gender equality initiatives reflect her ongoing commitment to the cause.

She has been a vocal advocate for women to be given the same respect and recognition as their male counterparts in all aspects of broadcasting and sports journalism. Through her public speaking, Hazel continues to raise important issues regarding gender discrimination, pay equity, and the representation of women in the media.

CHAPTER 9

Legacy and Impact

Influence on Modern Broadcasting

Hazel Irvine has had a profound impact on modern broadcasting, particularly within the realm of sports media. Her career has spanned several decades, and during that time, she has contributed significantly to the evolution of how sports are presented, discussed, and consumed by audiences. From her pioneering work as a female broadcaster in a traditionally male-dominated field to her ongoing efforts to shape the future of sports media, Hazel Irvine's influence has been both deep and lasting. Below are key ways in which she has influenced modern broadcasting:

1. Breaking Gender Barriers in Sports Broadcasting

As one of the leading female sports broadcasters in the UK, Hazel Irvine has had a monumental role in breaking gender barriers within the broadcasting industry. When she began her career, the sports media landscape was overwhelmingly male, and few women occupied key roles in sports commentary and live sports presentation. Hazel, as one of the few women in such prominent positions, paved the way for future generations of female broadcasters by proving that women could provide insightful commentary and lead coverage of major sporting events.

Her success in this field has inspired countless women to pursue careers in sports media, contributing to a gradual but significant shift toward gender equality in sports broadcasting. As a result, women now hold more prominent positions in sports commentary, analysis, and presenting roles. Hazel's long-standing career and accomplishments have helped normalize the presence of women in the sports media industry.

2. Impact on the Coverage of Women's Sports

Throughout her career, Hazel Irvine has been an outspoken advocate for the visibility and representation of women's sports in the media. As the demand for gender equality in broadcasting has grown, Hazel has championed the cause of increased media coverage for female athletes and women's sports events. She has played a pivotal role in giving more airtime to women's competitions, such as women's golf, tennis, and the Winter Olympics, where she has provided expert commentary and hosted coverage.

Her advocacy for women's sports has not only resulted in greater media exposure for these events but has also influenced the growing appreciation and recognition of female athletes. By elevating the profile of women's sports, Hazel has contributed to the movement toward a more inclusive and balanced portrayal of sports across various media platforms.

3. Enhancing the Presentation of Live Sports

Hazel Irvine has helped redefine how live sports coverage is presented, particularly in terms of quality analysis and expert commentary. Her deep knowledge of sports, combined with her ability to deliver commentary with clarity and insight, has raised the standard for live sports broadcasting. Hazel's commentary is not only accurate but also engaging, and her expertise has been instrumental in delivering a more dynamic and professional sports presentation.

Her work in live broadcasting during major events such as the Olympic Games, The Open Championship, and World Snooker Championships has set a high benchmark for sports journalism, influencing how other broadcasters approach live sports coverage. Hazel's ability to balance thorough analysis with approachable and entertaining commentary has inspired a new wave of sports broadcasters to strive for both depth and relatability in their own work.

4. Pioneering Roles for Women in Commentary

Hazel Irvine has been a trailblazer in securing commentary roles for women, particularly in sports where women were traditionally sidelined. While many female broadcasters have held presenting roles, it was rare for women to be seen as experts in the commentary booth for sports like golf, snooker, or even the Winter Olympics. Hazel, however, has broken this mold by providing expert commentary on these events, earning the respect of audiences and peers alike for her deep knowledge of the sports she covers.

By securing commentary positions alongside male colleagues, Hazel has helped to challenge long-standing gender norms in sports broadcasting and has opened doors for other women to follow in her footsteps. This has allowed more women to be recognized for their knowledge and expertise in a variety of sports, paving the way for greater gender parity in broadcast commentary roles.

5. Use of Technology and Digital Media

Hazel Irvine has adapted seamlessly to the digital transformation of broadcasting, embracing new technologies to enhance the viewer experience. The use of interactive platforms, social media, and digital streaming services has revolutionized the way sports are consumed. Hazel has played a role in this shift by contributing to online broadcasts and engaging with audiences through social media platforms. Her presence on digital platforms has made her more accessible to viewers and has allowed her to reach a younger, tech-savvy audience.

As sports coverage has increasingly moved online, Hazel's adaptability to new technologies has allowed her to maintain a strong presence in an evolving broadcasting landscape. Her use of digital tools for engaging with fans and delivering content has helped shape the future of how sports media is distributed and consumed in the digital age.

6. A Voice for Diversity and Inclusion

Hazel Irvine's influence extends beyond gender equality to include a broader commitment to diversity and inclusion in the media. She has been an advocate for better representation of ethnic minorities and marginalized communities within sports media, believing that a diverse range of voices leads to more accurate and engaging coverage of sports. Hazel has supported initiatives aimed at diversifying the sports media industry and increasing the representation of people from different backgrounds in key roles.

Her ongoing commitment to diversity has helped raise awareness about the importance of representation in media, and her support for inclusive policies has contributed to making sports broadcasting more reflective of the diverse audiences it serves.

7. Shaping Future Careers in Broadcasting

Hazel Irvine's career has had a lasting impact on those entering the broadcasting industry, particularly those pursuing careers in sports journalism. Her mentorship and public support of young female broadcasters have inspired many to enter the profession and challenge the existing norms. By actively engaging in mentoring programs and public speaking engagements, Hazel has helped guide the next generation of sports journalists, providing advice on how to succeed in an industry that is still working toward achieving full equality.

Her influence on new talent is part of a larger movement to reshape the future of broadcasting by empowering the next generation to break new ground in areas where women, ethnic minorities, and other underrepresented groups have been historically marginalized.

Inspirational Figure for Aspiring Journalists

Hazel Irvine stands as a beacon of inspiration for aspiring journalists, particularly those aiming to break into the competitive world of sports broadcasting. Her career is a testament to perseverance, skill, and the power of challenging norms, and she has become a role model for individuals from all backgrounds who aspire to follow in her footsteps. Below are the key aspects of why Hazel Irvine serves as such an influential and inspiring figure for the next generation of journalists.

1. Breaking Barriers in a Male-Dominated Field

One of the most remarkable aspects of Hazel Irvine's career is her trailblazing role in a predominantly male-dominated field. When she began her career, sports broadcasting was largely exclusive to men, with few women able to attain top-level roles. Hazel not only broke into this arena but also excelled, carving out a space for herself as a trusted commentator, presenter, and host of major sports events.

Her ability to rise to prominence in an industry that historically sidelined women in authoritative positions has shown aspiring journalists that gender should never be a barrier to success. Hazel's career sends a powerful message: with dedication, expertise, and passion, anyone can overcome obstacles and achieve success, regardless of gender.

2. Pioneering in Commentary and Reporting

In a time when women were often confined to roles as presenters or reporters rather than commentators, Hazel Irvine defied expectations by becoming a leading sports commentator. Her expertise in a variety of sports, such as golf, snooker, and the Olympics, has proved that knowledge and analysis are just as important as presentation skills in sports journalism. She has demonstrated that women can not only be the face of sports but can also be seen as credible, authoritative voices in the commentary box.

Aspiring journalists can look to Hazel as an example of how developing in-depth knowledge of a subject can help individuals carve a unique space for themselves in their chosen fields. Hazel's ability to seamlessly blend insight with on-screen charisma serves as a lesson to young journalists that expertise and authenticity are vital to making a lasting impact in the industry.

3. Resilience and Perseverance

Hazel Irvine's career trajectory is a story of resilience and perseverance. She faced challenges in an industry where the opportunities for women were limited, but she continued to work tirelessly to prove herself capable of covering high-profile events and providing top-tier commentary. Her determination is especially important for aspiring journalists, as it demonstrates that success doesn't come easily. Instead, it is earned through continuous effort, overcoming adversity, and maintaining high standards of work.

Her ability to navigate a long and successful career, despite the challenges she faced as a woman in sports media, serves as a powerful lesson for young journalists about the importance of perseverance in the face of obstacles. Hazel's journey proves that success is often not immediate but can be the result of years of hard work and dedication.

4. Advocating for Equality and Diversity

Hazel Irvine has long been an advocate for gender equality, diversity, and inclusion within broadcasting and sports media. She has been an outspoken supporter of women's rights in the industry, promoting equal opportunities for women to occupy high-profile broadcasting and commentary roles. She has also been vocal in supporting the increased visibility and representation of female athletes in sports media.

Aspiring journalists who share Hazel's values can look to her as a role model for how to use one's platform for good. Her advocacy work encourages young journalists to not only focus on their individual careers but also to stand up for the issues they care about, whether it's advocating for gender equality, challenging stereotypes, or working to ensure fair representation in the media.

5. Mentorship and Support for Young Talent

In addition to her own accomplishments, Hazel has been actively involved in mentoring young journalists and female broadcasters who aspire to follow in her footsteps. She regularly shares her experiences and offers guidance on how to navigate the media industry. This commitment to helping others succeed reflects her understanding that mentorship is crucial in fostering the next generation of media professionals.

Aspiring journalists can learn from Hazel the importance of giving back to their community and assisting others in their professional growth. Her willingness to guide newcomers to the industry, particularly women, reinforces the idea that success is not just about personal achievement but also about helping others achieve their potential.

6. Adapting to Change and Embracing Digital Innovation

The media landscape has undergone significant changes in recent years, with the rise of digital platforms and social media altering how journalism is consumed. Hazel Irvine has adapted to these changes, embracing new technologies and digital tools to connect with audiences and enhance her work. By moving with the times and staying ahead of the curve, Hazel has remained a relevant and influential figure in the broadcasting world.

For aspiring journalists, Hazel's ability to embrace technological advancements and adapt her work to new platforms is an invaluable lesson. It shows that, in the ever-changing media world, journalists must remain flexible and willing to learn in order to stay ahead in a competitive industry.

7. The Power of Authenticity

Throughout her career, Hazel Irvine has remained authentic and true to herself. She is known for her clear, engaging, and honest commentary, which resonates with audiences because it reflects her true passion for sports. This authenticity has been key to her success and has contributed to her popularity and longevity in the industry.

Aspiring journalists can take inspiration from Hazel's example by understanding that authenticity is crucial for building a strong connection with audiences. Whether in front of the camera or behind the scenes, remaining true to one's values and passions will help journalists develop a genuine rapport with viewers and create content that resonates.

8. Impacting Future Generations

Hazel Irvine's legacy will undoubtedly influence future generations of journalists, particularly those looking to break into sports broadcasting. Her career is proof that with talent, hard work, and a strong sense of purpose, anyone can achieve success in an industry that is often difficult to break into. She has set a standard for excellence in sports journalism and continues to inspire young journalists to strive for excellence, integrity, and professionalism in their work.

Her career serves as an example that the path to success is not always easy but can be incredibly rewarding for those who are determined and passionate about their work. For aspiring journalists, Hazel's journey offers both practical and emotional guidance for building a fulfilling career in broadcasting.

Conclusion

Summary of Achievements

Hazel Irvine is a pioneering figure in the world of sports broadcasting, widely recognized for her contributions to the industry, particularly for breaking gender barriers and shaping the future of sports media. Below is a summary of her notable achievements:

1. Trailblazer for Women in Sports Broadcasting

Hazel became one of the first prominent female sports broadcasters in the UK, challenging the male-dominated industry and opening doors for future generations of women in media. Her success in securing top-tier roles, including commentary and live event hosting, set a precedent for gender equality in sports broadcasting.

2. Pioneering Commentary and Reporting

She made significant strides in securing expert commentary roles in traditionally male-dominated sports such as golf, snooker, and the Olympics, becoming one of the leading female voices in these fields. Hazel's insightful analysis has raised the bar for sports journalism and presented a new standard for the quality of commentary.

3. Coverage of Major Sporting Events

Throughout her career, Hazel has been a key figure in the BBC's coverage of global sporting events, including the Olympic Games, The Open Championship, and World Snooker Championships. Her comprehensive coverage has made her a staple of major sports broadcasts, further establishing her as a trusted and authoritative presence in the field.

4. Advocacy for Women's Sports

Hazel has been a strong advocate for the increased visibility of women's sports, dedicating her platform to promoting female athletes and advocating for better representation in media. Her efforts have contributed to the growing recognition of women's sports and helped foster greater media coverage for female competitions.

5. Industry Recognition

Throughout her career, Hazel Irvine has received accolades for her work, solidifying her reputation as one of the leading figures in sports journalism. She has been recognized not only for her expertise and professionalism but also for her influence in breaking down barriers for women in sports media.

6. Mentorship and Advocacy for Diversity

Hazel has mentored young journalists and advocated for greater diversity and inclusion within the industry. She has been a vocal supporter of equal opportunities for women and marginalized groups in sports broadcasting, contributing to the ongoing evolution of the industry toward greater inclusivity.

7. Adaptation to Digital Media

Hazel has embraced the changing landscape of sports media by adapting to digital platforms and social media, ensuring her relevance in the modern broadcasting era. Her ability to engage with audiences through new technologies has positioned her as a forward-thinking leader in the industry.

8. Continued Influence and Legacy

With a career spanning decades, Hazel Irvine has become a role model for aspiring sports journalists, particularly women. Her legacy is one of perseverance, excellence, and breaking down barriers, inspiring the next generation of broadcasters to follow in her footsteps.

Future Prospects and Ongoing Influence

Hazel Irvine's career has left an indelible mark on the world of sports broadcasting, and as she continues to evolve in her role, her influence remains powerful. Looking ahead, her ongoing contributions to the media industry and her legacy offer several exciting prospects for the future:

1. Continued Leadership in Sports Broadcasting

Hazel Irvine is likely to remain a central figure in sports broadcasting, continuing to serve as a trusted commentator and presenter for major events. As one of the most experienced and respected figures in the field, she is well-positioned to take on even more prominent roles, perhaps expanding her reach to new sports or international events. Given her vast expertise, she is a prime candidate to remain a leading voice in live sports coverage, providing both in-depth analysis and a connection to the audience that makes her broadcasts stand out.

2. Mentorship and Advocacy for the Next Generation

As a pioneering female figure in the industry, Hazel is expected to continue her efforts in mentoring the next generation of broadcasters, especially young women pursuing careers in sports journalism. With her deep commitment to increasing diversity and inclusion in sports media, she will likely focus on creating opportunities for underrepresented groups in the industry. Hazel's guidance and advocacy for women in media will continue to inspire those seeking to follow in her footsteps, ensuring that her influence extends far beyond her own career.

3. Expanding Digital and Online Presence

Given the growing significance of digital media and the rise of online platforms, Hazel Irvine's influence is poised to grow in the digital realm.

She may expand her presence on social media, streaming platforms, or digital podcasts, providing expert commentary and analysis in new formats that appeal to younger, tech-savvy audiences. Her ability to embrace emerging technologies, as demonstrated throughout her career, will likely ensure she remains at the forefront of the evolving broadcasting landscape.

4. Advocacy for Women's Sports and Equality

Hazel has long been a passionate advocate for greater visibility of women's sports and gender equality within the media. In the future, she is likely to continue to champion these causes, pushing for more media coverage and equal representation of women's competitions. Her advocacy efforts could extend to mentoring female athletes, helping them gain the media recognition they deserve, or even creating platforms that highlight the achievements of female athletes in all sports.

5. Involvement in High-Profile Sports Projects

As sports broadcasting continues to expand globally, Hazel may take on more international projects, such as covering major global events like the FIFA World Cup, the Commonwealth Games, or the Paralympics. Her expertise and international appeal could allow her to become a leading figure in international sports media, providing critical commentary and insights into a wider array of sports events on the world stage.

6. Legacy as a Role Model for Aspiring Journalists

Hazel's ongoing influence will continue to shape the careers of aspiring sports journalists, particularly women, for many years to come. As one of the most visible and respected figures in the industry, her legacy as a trailblazer for women in broadcasting will inspire future generations of journalists. Her example of hard work, resilience, and commitment to excellence will serve as a guide for young journalists entering the field.

7. Expanding Roles in Media Beyond Sports

Though sports broadcasting remains her core focus, Hazel may also take on more general broadcasting roles or delve into other areas of media. Her success as a presenter and her in-depth knowledge of various fields could see her expanding into other genres of television or radio, continuing her evolution as a versatile and influential figure in the wider broadcasting industry.

8. Contributions to Charitable and Advocacy Efforts

Hazel's advocacy for women's equality and diversity in broadcasting will continue to influence her ongoing work in charitable initiatives and industry reform. She may deepen her involvement in philanthropic causes, including those related to education, women's rights, and equal opportunities in media. Her involvement in initiatives that support diversity in sports and broadcasting may become a central focus as she continues to leverage her platform for positive change.